PAWSITIVELY POPULAR

How to Make Your Pet Famous, and Profitable, on Instagram

Introduction

Instagram has become one of the most popular social media platforms for sharing photos and videos of our daily lives, including our pets. From cute kittens to playful puppies, pets have taken over Instagram, and pet owners have found a unique opportunity to showcase their furry friends and even turn them into celebrities.

If you are a pet owner looking to make your pet famous on Instagram, you've come to the right place. In this book, we will guide you through the process of building a successful pet influencer brand on Instagram, from creating a strong profile to engaging with your followers and growing your audience.

We will share with you our best tips and tricks for creating compelling content, building a loyal following, and partnering with brands for sponsored posts. We'll also discuss how to navigate the ever-changing Instagram algorithm and stay on top of the latest trends in the pet influencer world.

Throughout this book, we will provide practical advice and examples from successful pet influencers who have built their brands from scratch and turned their pets into Instagram stars. We'll show you how they have leveraged their pet's unique personalities and quirks to capture the hearts of their followers and turn their passion for pets into a lucrative career.
Whether you are just starting out on Instagram or have already built a following but want to take your pet's influencer brand to the next level, this book is for you. Let's get started and make your pet the next Instagram sensation!

TABLE OF CONTENTS

Chapter 1:

UNDERSTANDING THE POWER OF INSTAGRAM FOR PET FAME

2

THE RISE OF PET INFLUENCERS ON SOCIAL MEDIA

Instagram has seen a surge in the number of pet accounts over the past few years. It's not just celebrity pets like Grumpy Cat and Boo the Pomeranian anymore - everyday pet owners are turning their furry friends into Instagram stars with millions of followers. This rise of pet influencers is due to several factors, including the increasing popularity of social media, the rise of the pet industry, and the emotional connections that people have with their pets.

As a pet owner, this trend presents an opportunity for you to showcase your pet's unique personality and share their antics with the world. By building a following on Instagram, you can also leverage your pet's fame to work with brands, monetize their account, and even make a difference for animal causes and charities.

However, it's important to note that building a successful pet influencer brand takes time, effort, and dedication. This book will guide you through the process of making your pet famous on Instagram, from setting up their account to building a community of followers and beyond. By understanding the power of Instagram for pet fame and the potential benefits, you can take the first step towards turning your furry friend into a social media star.

3

THE BENEFITS OF HAVING A FAMOUS PET ON INSTAGRAM

Having a famous pet on Instagram can bring many benefits to both you and your furry friend. Some of the main benefits include:

1. **INCREASED VISIBILITY AND RECOGNITION:** By having a large following on Instagram, your pet can become a recognizable figure in the pet influencer community. This can lead to opportunities for collaborations with brands, media appearances, and even product endorsements.

2. **MONETIZATION OPPORTUNITIES**: With a large following, your pet's Instagram account can become a source of income through sponsored posts, affiliate marketing, and selling merchandise. This can be a great way to supplement your income and turn your pet's fame into a business.

3. **BUILDING A COMMUNITY:** Pet influencers on Instagram often have dedicated fans who follow their every move and engage with their content. This can create a sense of community and support around your pet, and even lead to meet-and-greets with fans.

4. **SPREADING AWARENESS FOR ANIMAL CAUSES:** With a large platform, you can use your pet's Instagram account to raise awareness for animal causes and charities that you care about. This can help make a positive impact on the world and give your pet's fame a greater purpose.

While fame on Instagram may not be for every pet, understanding the potential benefits can help you decide if it's worth pursuing. By building a successful pet influencer brand, you can not only bring joy to your followers but also open up opportunities for your pet and make a difference for animal causes.

5

THE DIFFERENT TYPES OF PET ACCOUNTS ON INSTAGRAM

On Instagram, there are many different types of pet accounts that you can create to showcase your furry friend's personality and charm. Some of the most popular types of pet accounts include:

1. **LIFESTYLE ACCOUNTS:** These accounts feature your pet's daily life, showcasing their personality, routines, and adventures. They often include a mix of photos and videos, with captions that capture your pet's unique quirks and personality.

2. **RESCUE ACCOUNTS:** These accounts highlight pets that are in need of forever homes. By sharing photos and videos of adoptable pets, you can help them find loving families and raise awareness for animal rescues.

3. **HUMOR ACCOUNTS:** These accounts focus on making people laugh with funny photos and videos of your pet. They often include witty captions and memes that showcase your pet's comedic talents.

4. **EDUCATIONAL ACCOUNTS:** These accounts share information and tips about pet care, training, and behavior. By sharing your knowledge and experience as a pet owner, you can help others learn more about their own pets and build a community of pet enthusiasts.

5. **BRAND ACCOUNTS:** These accounts promote a specific product or service related to pets, such as pet food, toys, or grooming products. They often feature sponsored content and partnerships with other brands in the pet industry.

Deciding on the type of account that best suits your pet's personality and your goals for their Instagram fame is an important first step in building a successful pet influencer brand. By understanding the different types of pet accounts on Instagram, you can create content that resonates with your followers and helps your pet stand out in a crowded market.

Chapter 2:

SETTING UP YOUR PET'S INSTAGRAM ACCOUNT

8

CHOOSING A HANDLE AND PROFILE PICTURE

When setting up your pet's Instagram account, the first step is to choose a handle and profile picture that represent your pet's personality and brand. Here are some tips to keep in mind:

1. **KEEP IT SIMPLE AND EASY TO REMEMBER:** Choose a handle that is easy to spell and remember. Avoid using numbers or special characters that can make it hard to find your account.

2. **INCORPORATE YOUR PET'S NAME:** Your pet's name should be a part of the handle to make it easy for people to find your account when searching for your pet.

3. **USE A CLEAR AND RECOGNIZABLE PROFILE PICTURE:** Your pet's profile picture should be clear and recognizable, with your pet's face as the focus. Avoid using blurry or low-quality images.

4. **MAKE IT CONSISTENT WITH YOUR BRAND:** Your handle and profile picture should be consistent with the type of account you have decided to create. If you have a humorous account, for example, choose a profile picture that reflects your pet's comedic personality.

5. **ADD A BIO:** Your pet's Instagram bio should be short and catchy, highlighting your pet's personality and the type of content you will be posting.

By taking the time to choose a handle and profile picture that accurately represent your pet's brand, you can make it easier for people to find and follow your pet on Instagram. This will be a crucial step in building a loyal following and achieving Instagram fame for your furry friend.

WRITING A BIO THAT CAPTURES YOUR PET'S PERSONALITY

Your pet's Instagram bio is a short and concise introduction to your pet's brand. It should showcase your pet's personality, provide essential information, and give your followers a reason to engage with your content. Here are some tips to help you craft a compelling bio for your pet's account:

1. **KEEP IT SHORT AND SWEET:** Instagram bios have a 150 character limit, so keep your bio short and to the point. Highlight the most important aspects of your pet's personality and brand.

2. **USE EMOJIS:** Emojis are a fun and visual way to add personality to your bio. Use them to convey your pet's personality, likes, and interests.

3. **INCLUDE ESSENTIAL INFORMATION:** Your bio should include essential information about your pet, such as their name, breed, age, and location. This will help your followers get to know your pet better.

4. **HIGHLIGHT YOUR PET'S UNIQUE FEATURES:** What sets your pet apart from others? Highlight your pet's unique features or talents in your bio to make them stand out.

5. **CALL-TO-ACTION:** End your bio with a call-to-action that encourages your followers to engage with your content. This can be a simple invitation to follow your account, or a request to tag your pet in their photos.

6. **USE KEYWORDS:** Use relevant keywords in your bio that reflect the type of content you will be sharing. This will make it easier for people to find your account when searching for specific types of pets or content.

Remember, your pet's Instagram bio is often the first impression that people will have of your pet's account. Make it compelling, informative, and reflective of your pet's unique personality to help your pet stand out and build a loyal following.

CREATING A CONTENT STRATEGY FOR YOUR PET'S ACCOUNT

Once you have set up your pet's Instagram account, the next step is to create a content strategy that will help you achieve your goals for your pet's fame. Here are some tips for creating a content strategy:

1. **DEFINE YOUR BRAND:** Determine the type of content you will be sharing on your pet's account and the brand image you want to project. This will help you choose the right type of content that resonates with your followers.

2. **POST CONSISTENTLY:** Posting consistently is key to building a following on Instagram. Determine how often you will post and create a schedule to ensure you stick to it.

3. **USE HIGH-QUALITY IMAGES AND VIDEOS:** Instagram is a visual platform, so it's important to use high-quality images and videos that showcase your pet in the best possible way.

4. **ENGAGE WITH YOUR FOLLOWERS:** Engage with your followers by responding to comments, asking for feedback, and hosting giveaways. This will help you build a loyal community around your pet's account.

5. **USE RELEVANT HASHTAGS:** Hashtags help people find your content on Instagram, so it's important to use relevant hashtags that reflect the type of content you are sharing.

6. **COLLABORATE WITH OTHER ACCOUNTS:** Collaborating with other pet accounts can help you reach new audiences and grow your following.

By creating a content strategy that is aligned with your goals for your pet's fame, you can build a strong and engaged following on Instagram. Remember to be consistent, engaging, and creative with your content to help your pet stand out in a crowded market.

Chapter 3:

TAKING GREAT PHOTOS AND VIDEOS OF YOUR PET

THE BASICS OF PET PHOTOGRAPHY

Good photography is essential for creating compelling content on Instagram. Whether you are using a professional camera or a smartphone, here are some basic photography tips that will help you capture the perfect shot of your pet:

1. **LIGHTING:** Lighting is one of the most important factors in photography. Avoid using the flash as it can cause red-eye and harsh shadows. Instead, try to use natural light, such as sunlight or soft light from a window.

2. **COMPOSITION:** Composition refers to how the elements in your photo are arranged. When taking a photo of your pet, try to keep them the focal point of the photo. Use the rule of thirds to create a balanced and visually appealing composition. For example, if your pet is facing left, position them to the right of the frame.

3. **FOCUS:** Make sure your pet's eyes are in focus as they are often the most expressive part of their face. Use the autofocus feature on your camera or tap on your pet's eyes on the smartphone screen to ensure they are in focus.

4. **ANGLES:** Experiment with different angles to add variety to your photos. For example, getting down to your pet's eye level can create a more intimate and engaging photo.

5. **PATIENCE:** Patience is key when photographing pets. Take your time and wait for the right moment to capture the perfect shot. Treats or toys can be used to grab your pet's attention and encourage them to pose.

Remember, photography is an art, and it takes time and practice to master. Don't be afraid to experiment with different techniques and angles to capture your pet's unique personality. With a little patience and practice, you can create stunning photos that will make your pet famous on Instagram.

TIPS FOR CAPTURING YOUR PET'S UNIQUE PERSONALITY

Capturing your pet's unique personality is one of the best ways to make them stand out on Instagram. Here are some tips to help you capture your pet's unique traits and characteristics:

1. **SHOWCASE THEIR INTERESTS:** Every pet has their own unique interests and hobbies. Whether your pet loves playing with toys or enjoys long walks in the park, try to capture their interests in your photos and videos. For example, if your pet loves playing with balls, capture them in action with their favorite toy.

2. **SHOW THEIR EMOTIONS:** Pets are known for their expressive faces and body language. Try to capture their emotions in your photos, whether they are happy, sad, or playful. For example, if your pet is feeling playful, capture them in action with a big smile on their face.

3. **HIGHLIGHT THEIR QUIRKS:** Every pet has their own unique quirks and habits. Whether your pet has a funny way of sitting or a cute little tail wag, try to capture their quirks in your photos and videos. For example, if your pet has a funny way of sleeping, capture them in a cute and funny sleeping position.

4. **CAPTURE THEIR INTERACTIONS:** Pets are social creatures, and capturing their interactions with other pets or people can be a great way to showcase their personality. For example, if your pet loves playing with other dogs, capture them in a fun and playful group photo.

5. **USE CAPTIONS:** Captions can be a great way to showcase your pet's personality and add context to your photos and videos. Use witty and funny captions to show off your pet's playful side, or use emotional captions to showcase their sensitive side.

Remember, your pet's unique personality is what makes them special, and capturing it in your photos and videos is essential to making them famous on Instagram. Use these tips to showcase your pet's unique traits and characteristics and make them stand out from the crowd.

EDITING AND ENHANCING YOUR PET'S PHOTOS AND VIDEOS

After you have captured the perfect photo or video of your pet, the next step is to edit and enhance it to make it stand out on Instagram. Here are some tips for editing and enhancing your pet's photos and videos:

1. **CHOOSE THE RIGHT APP:** There are many photo and video editing apps available, so it's important to choose one that is easy to use and has the features you need. Popular apps for editing photos include VSCO, Adobe Lightroom, and Snapseed, while popular video editing apps include iMovie and InShot.

2. **ADJUST THE BRIGHTNESS AND CONTRAST:** Adjusting the brightness and contrast can help to make your photo or video more vibrant and eye-catching. Be careful not to overdo it, as this can make the image look unrealistic.

3. **CROP AND STRAIGHTEN:** Cropping and straightening your photo can help to create a more balanced and visually appealing composition. Use the rule of thirds to guide your cropping, and ensure that your pet remains the focal point of the image.

4. **ADD FILTERS:** Adding a filter can help to give your photo or video a consistent look and feel. Experiment with different filters to find one that enhances the colors and tones in your image.

5. **ADD TEXT AND GRAPHICS:** Adding text and graphics can help to add context and personality to your photo or video. Use text to add a funny caption or a personal message, or use graphics to highlight your pet's name or breed.

6. **USE SOUND EFFECTS AND MUSIC:** Adding sound effects and music to your videos can help to create a more engaging and immersive experience. Use sound effects to enhance your pet's actions or reactions, or use music to create a specific mood or atmosphere.

Remember, editing and enhancing your pet's photos and videos is a great way to make them stand out on Instagram. Use these tips to create stunning and eye-catching content that showcases your pet's unique personality and traits.

Chapter 4:

CREATING COMPELLING CAPTIONS AND HASHTAGS

WRITING CAPTIONS THAT ENGAGE YOUR AUDIENCE

When it comes to making your pet famous on Instagram, writing captions that engage your audience is just as important as capturing great photos and videos. Here are some tips for writing captions that will keep your audience engaged and coming back for more:

1. **KEEP IT SHORT AND SWEET:** Instagram captions have a limit of 2,200 characters, but that doesn't mean you need to use them all. In fact, shorter captions are often more effective at engaging your audience. Aim for a caption that is around 100-150 characters in length.

2. **USE EMOJIS:** Emojis are a great way to add personality and emotion to your captions. Use them to express your pet's emotions or to add a playful touch to your caption.

3. **USE A CALL-TO-ACTION:** A call-to-action is a statement that encourages your audience to take a specific action, such as "Tag a friend who loves dogs!" or "Follow us for more cute pet photos!" Using a call-to-action can help to increase engagement and encourage your audience to interact with your content.

4. **TELL A STORY:** Captions are a great way to tell a story about your pet, whether it's a funny anecdote or a heartwarming moment. Use your caption to add context to your photo or video and to showcase your pet's unique personality.

5. **USE HUMOR:** Humor is a great way to engage your audience and add a lighthearted touch to your content. Use puns, jokes, or witty comments to show off your pet's playful side.

6. **BE AUTHENTIC:** Authenticity is key to building a loyal following on Instagram. Use your captions to showcase your genuine love and affection for your pet, and to share your personal experiences as a pet owner.

Remember, writing captions that engage your audience is an essential part of making your pet famous on Instagram. Use these tips to create captions that showcase your pet's personality and traits and to keep your audience engaged and coming back for more.

USING HASHTAGS TO REACH NEW FOLLOWERS

Using hashtags is a powerful way to reach new followers on Instagram. When used correctly, hashtags can help your content reach a wider audience and increase your visibility on the platform. Here are some tips for using hashtags to reach new followers:

1. **USE RELEVANT HASHTAGS:** When selecting hashtags, make sure to choose ones that are relevant to your pet and the content you are posting. This will help your content reach the right audience and increase the chances of new followers discovering your account. For example, if you are posting a photo of your cat, consider using hashtags like #catsofinstagram, #cutekittens, or #meow.

2. **USE A MIX OF POPULAR AND NICHE HASHTAGS:** While popular hashtags like #petsofinstagram or #dogsofinstagram can help your content reach a wider audience, they can also be highly competitive. Consider using a mix of popular and niche hashtags to increase your chances of being discovered. Niche hashtags like #rescuepetsofinstagram or #instapetbird are more specific and can help you reach a highly engaged audience.

3. **RESEARCH HASHTAGS:** Before using hashtags, it's important to research them to ensure they are appropriate and effective. You can use tools like Hashtagify or Instagram's built-in search feature to find relevant and popular hashtags.

4. **CREATE YOUR OWN HASHTAG:** Creating your own branded hashtag is a great way to build your brand and encourage user-generated content. For example, you can create a hashtag that includes your pet's name, such as #BuddytheBeagle, and encourage your followers to use it when posting photos of their own pets.

5. **USE HASHTAGS IN MODERATION:** While hashtags are an effective way to reach new followers, it's important not to overdo it. Instagram allows up to 30 hashtags per post, but using too many can make your captions look cluttered and spammy. Aim for 5-10 relevant and effective hashtags per post.

Remember, using hashtags is an effective way to reach new followers on Instagram. Use relevant, popular, and niche hashtags to increase your visibility on the platform and encourage new followers to discover your content.

COLLABORATING WITH OTHER PET ACCOUNTS TO BOOST YOUR PET'S VISIBILITY

Collaborating with other pet accounts on Instagram is a great way to increase your pet's visibility and reach new followers. Here are some tips for collaborating with other pet accounts:

1. **FIND ACCOUNTS WITH SIMILAR AUDIENCES:** When looking for accounts to collaborate with, make sure to find ones with a similar target audience. This will ensure that your collaboration is relevant to both of your audiences and increases the chances of gaining new followers. For example, if you have a cat, you might want to collaborate with other cat accounts or pet accounts that focus on cats.

2. **REACH OUT TO OTHER ACCOUNTS:** Once you have identified accounts to collaborate with, reach out to them with a proposal for collaboration. You can suggest things like co-posting, shoutouts, or even guest posts. Make sure to be clear about what you are offering and what you hope to gain from the collaboration.

3. **FOLLOW UP AND ENGAGE:** Once you have established a collaboration, make sure to follow up and engage with the other account's content. This

will help to strengthen the relationship and increase the chances of future collaborations.

4. **BE CREATIVE:** Collaboration doesn't have to be limited to simply co-posting or shoutouts. Get creative and come up with unique ideas that will engage both of your audiences. For example, you can create a joint Instagram Live session, host a Q&A with both pets, or create a fun challenge that both of your pets can participate in.

Remember, collaborating with other pet accounts is a great way to increase your pet's visibility and reach new followers. Find accounts with a similar audience, reach out with a clear proposal, follow up and engage, and get creative with your collaboration ideas.

Chapter 5:

BUILDING YOUR PET'S INSTAGRAM FOLLOWING

STRATEGIES FOR ATTRACTING NEW FOLLOWERS

While collaborating with other pet accounts and using hashtags can help you reach new followers, there are other strategies you can use to attract them. Here are some practical tips:

1. **POST CONSISTENTLY:** Consistency is key on Instagram. Make sure to post regularly and at the right times to maximize your reach. You can use analytics tools to determine when your followers are most active and schedule your posts accordingly.

2. **USE ENGAGING CAPTIONS:** Captions are just as important as photos or videos. Use captions that are engaging and tell a story about your pet. You can ask questions, share anecdotes, or even add a call-to-action to encourage engagement.

3. **SHARE USER-GENERATED CONTENT:** Encourage your followers to share photos and videos of their pets and feature them on your account. This not only increases engagement but also helps to attract new followers who are interested in the content you're sharing.

4. **HOST GIVEAWAYS:** Host giveaways and contests to attract new followers and increase engagement. You can ask your followers to tag their friends and follow your account to enter the giveaway.

5. **CROSS-PROMOTE ON OTHER PLATFORMS:** Use other social media platforms to promote your pet's Instagram account. For example, you can share your pet's Instagram handle on your personal Facebook or Twitter accounts, or even create a TikTok account to showcase your pet's personality.

Remember, attracting new followers on Instagram takes time and effort. Post consistently, use engaging captions, share user-generated content, host giveaways, and cross-promote on other platforms to increase your pet's visibility and attract new followers.

ENGAGING WITH YOUR FOLLOWERS TO BUILD A COMMUNITY

Building a community of followers around your pet's Instagram account is essential for maintaining long-term success. Engaging with your followers not only helps to build a loyal following but also helps to increase engagement on your account. Here are some practical tips for engaging with your followers:

1. **RESPOND TO COMMENTS:** Responding to comments on your posts shows your followers that you appreciate their engagement and value their opinion. You can respond with a simple "thank you" or engage in a conversation by asking a follow-up question.

2. **HOST Q&A SESSIONS:** Host Q&A sessions on your Instagram stories or posts to give your followers the opportunity to ask questions about your pet. This not only helps to build a relationship with your followers but also gives you an opportunity to share more about your pet's personality and backstory.

3. **SHARE BEHIND-THE-SCENES CONTENT:** Share behind-the-scenes content of your pet's life to give your followers a glimpse into their world. This could be anything from a day at the park to a visit to the

vet. Sharing these moments helps to build a more personal connection with your followers.

4. **ASK FOR FEEDBACK:** Ask for feedback on your posts, captions, and overall account. This shows your followers that you value their opinion and are open to making changes based on their feedback.

5. **HOST INSTAGRAM LIVE SESSIONS:** Host Instagram Live sessions to connect with your followers in real-time. You can answer questions, share tips, and even collaborate with other pet accounts during these sessions.

Remember, engaging with your followers is essential for building a loyal community around your pet's Instagram account. Respond to comments, host Q&A sessions, share behind-the-scenes content, ask for feedback, and host Instagram Live sessions to build a strong relationship with your followers.

GROWING YOUR PET'S ACCOUNT WITH CONTESTS AND GIVEAWAYS

Contests and giveaways are a great way to grow your pet's Instagram account and engage with your followers. By offering something of value, such as a prize or discount code, you can encourage your followers to engage with your account and invite others to follow you. Here are some practical tips for running contests and giveaways:

1. **DEFINE YOUR GOALS:** Determine what you want to achieve with your contest or giveaway. Do you want to increase engagement, followers, or sales? Once you define your goals, you can tailor your contest or giveaway to meet those goals.

2. **CHOOSE A PRIZE:** Choose a prize that is relevant to your audience and will motivate them to participate. The prize could be anything from a product related to your pet to a gift card to a popular pet store.

3. **DECIDE ON THE RULES:** Decide on the rules for your contest or giveaway, including how to enter, how the winner will be chosen, and when the contest or giveaway ends. Be sure to communicate the rules clearly to avoid confusion or disputes.

4. **PROMOTE YOUR CONTEST OR GIVEAWAY:** Promote your contest or giveaway across all of your social media channels to increase visibility and encourage participation. You can also collaborate with other pet accounts to expand your reach.

5. **FOLLOW THROUGH:** Once the contest or giveaway is over, be sure to follow through on your promises. Announce the winner, send the prize promptly, and thank your followers for participating.

Examples of contest and giveaway ideas include a photo contest where followers can submit pictures of their own pets, a trivia contest about your pet's breed or personality, or a giveaway where followers must tag friends in the comments to enter. By running contests and giveaways, you can attract new followers, engage with your current audience, and promote your pet's account.

Chapter 6:

MONETIZING YOUR PET'S INSTAGRAM FAME

UNDERSTANDING THE DIFFERENT WAYS TO MAKE MONEY FROM A PET'S INSTAGRAM ACCOUNT

If your pet's Instagram account has gained a substantial following, you may be wondering how you can monetize it. Here are some practical ways to make money from your pet's Instagram account:

1. **SPONSORED CONTENT:** Sponsored content involves working with brands or companies to promote their products or services on your pet's Instagram account. You may receive a flat fee or a commission for each sale made through your unique affiliate link. Sponsored content can include sponsored posts, stories, or even entire campaigns.

EXAMPLE: A pet food brand may reach out to your pet's account to promote their new line of pet food. They may pay you a flat fee for a sponsored post, or offer you a commission for each sale made through your unique affiliate link.

2. **PRODUCT SALES:** If your pet has a unique brand or following, you may consider creating and selling your own products, such as clothing or accessories, related to your pet. You can promote and sell these products directly through your pet's Instagram account.

EXAMPLE: If your pet is a well-known fashionista, you may consider creating and selling your own line of pet clothing or accessories, such as bow ties or hats.

3. **BRAND PARTNERSHIPS:** Similar to sponsored content, brand partnerships involve collaborating with brands to create long-term relationships that benefit both parties. You may receive a regular fee or commission for promoting their products or services over an extended period of time.

EXAMPLE: A pet grooming company may partner with your pet's account to promote their products on an ongoing basis. In exchange, you may receive a regular commission or fee for promoting their brand.

4. **AFFILIATE MARKETING:** Affiliate marketing involves promoting other brands' products or services on your pet's Instagram account and earning a commission for each sale made through your unique affiliate link.

EXAMPLE: A pet toy company may provide you with a unique affiliate link to their website. When you promote their products on your pet's Instagram account and followers make a purchase using your affiliate link, you earn a commission.

5. **DONATIONS:** If your pet has a large and dedicated following, you may consider setting up a donation page to receive support from your followers.

EXAMPLE: If your pet is a therapy dog or has overcome a serious illness, you may set up a donation page to receive support from your followers to help fund your pet's medical expenses or donate to a charitable cause related to your pet.

By understanding the different ways to make money from your pet's Instagram account, you can explore the options that work best for you and your pet's brand. It's important to remain authentic and transparent with your followers when promoting products or services, and only work with brands or companies that align with your values and your pet's brand.

WORKING WITH BRANDS TO PROMOTE PRODUCTS AND SERVICES

One of the most common ways to monetize a pet's Instagram account is by working with brands to promote their products or services. Brands are often looking for influencers with large following and high engagement ratess to help them reach their target audience. Here are some tips for working with brands:

1. **CHOOSE BRANDS THAT ALIGN WITH YOUR PET'S BRAND:** It's important to only promote products or services that fit with your pet's image and values. For example, if your pet is known for being eco-friendly, it wouldn't make sense to promote a brand that is known for its wasteful packaging.

2. **BE TRANSPARENT WITH YOUR AUDIENCE:** It's important to disclose when a post is sponsored or when you have received a product for free in exchange for a post. This helps to build trust with your audience and ensures that you are being transparent about any potential biases.

3. **NEGOTIATE FAIR COMPENSATION:** When working with brands, it's important to negotiate fair compensation for your time and effort. Consider factors such as the amount of work involved, the

value of the product or service being promoted, and your audience size and engagement rates.

4. **CREATE ENGAGING CONTENT:** When promoting a product or service, it's important to create engaging content that highlights the product's features and benefits. This could include photos or videos of your pet using or enjoying the product, or testimonials from you or your pet about why you love the product.

5. **TRACK YOUR RESULTS:** It's important to track the success of your brand collaborations to ensure that they are worth your time and effort. Keep track of metrics such as engagement rates, website clicks, and sales to determine the success of each collaboration.

EXAMPLE: Let's say your pet is a dog who loves to hike and explore the outdoors. You could partner with a brand that sells outdoor gear and create content that showcases your pet using their products on hikes or camping trips. You could create an engaging caption that highlights the benefits of the products, such as their durability and usefulness on outdoor adventures. You could also negotiate fair compensation for your time and effort, such as a set amount of money or free products from the brand. Finally, you could track the success of the collaboration by monitoring engagement rates and website clicks to determine if it was a worthwhile partnership.

BUILDING A SUCCESSFUL PET MERCHANDISE BRAND

Another way to monetize a pet's Instagram account is by building a successful pet merchandise brand. By creating and selling products that align with your pet's brand and image, you can generate a new source of income and further engage with your audience. Here are some tips for building a successful pet merchandise brand:

1. **IDENTIFY YOUR PET'S BRAND AND VALUES:** Before creating any products, it's important to identify your pet's brand and values. This includes factors such as their personality, interests, and the values that you want to promote. This will help you to create products that align with your pet's image and resonate with your audience.

2. **RESEARCH THE MARKET AND COMPETITION:** It's important to research the pet merchandise market and identify any gaps or opportunities for your brand. This includes researching your competition and identifying what sets your brand apart from theirs. You should also research the best platforms for selling your merchandise, such as your own website, Etsy, or Amazon.

3. **CREATE HIGH-QUALITY PRODUCTS:** When creating pet merchandise, it's important to prioritize quality over quantity. This means creating products that are durable, functional, and visually appealing. Consider hiring a professional designer or manufacturer to help bring your product ideas to life.

4. **PROMOTE YOUR PRODUCTS ON INSTAGRAM:** Once you have created your products, it's important to promote them on your pet's Instagram account. This includes creating engaging content that showcases your products and highlights their features and benefits. You could also consider running Instagram ads or partnering with other pet accounts to promote your brand.

5. **BUILD A LOYAL CUSTOMER BASE:** To build a successful pet merchandise brand, it's important to build a loyal customer base. This includes providing excellent customer service, offering promotions and discounts to repeat customers, and creating a strong brand image that resonates with your audience.

EXAMPLE: Let's say your pet is a cat who loves to lounge around the house and play with toys. You could create a line of cat toys and accessories that align with your cat's brand and values, such as toys made from sustainable materials or accessories that promote a healthy and active lifestyle. You could then promote your products on your cat's Instagram account by creating engaging content that showcases your products and highlights their features and benefits. You could also partner with other pet accounts or run Instagram ads to reach a wider audience. Finally, you could build a loyal customer base by providing excellent customer service and offering promotions and discounts to repeat customers.

Chapter 7:

MANAGING YOUR PET'S INSTAGRAM ACCOUNT FOR LONG-TERM SUCCESS

DEVELOPING A SUSTAINABLE CONTENT STRATEGY

Congratulations on creating a successful pet Instagram account! Now that you have built a following and established your pet's brand, it's time to think about developing a sustainable content strategy to keep your followers engaged and attract new ones. Here are some tips to help you with this process:

1. **DEFINE YOUR BRAND:** Before you start creating content, it's important to define your brand and what it stands for. What message do you want to convey to your followers? What sets your pet apart from others? Once you have a clear understanding of your brand, you can create content that aligns with it.

2. **PLAN YOUR CONTENT IN ADVANCE:** It's important to plan your content in advance to ensure that you're consistently posting high-quality and engaging content. Create a content calendar that includes upcoming holidays, events, and milestones, and plan your content accordingly. This will help you avoid the stress of last-minute content creation.

3. **MIX UP YOUR CONTENT:** While it's important to stay true to your brand, it's also essential to mix up your content to keep your followers engaged.

Experiment with different types of content, such as photos, videos, and stories. Try out new angles and perspectives to keep your content fresh.

4. **ENGAGE WITH YOUR FOLLOWERS:** Your followers are your biggest supporters, and engaging with them is crucial to building a strong community. Respond to comments and messages, and show your appreciation for their support. You can also ask for their feedback on your content to improve it.

5. **ANALYZE YOUR DATA:** To determine what content is resonating with your followers, you need to analyze your data regularly. Keep track of your engagement metrics, such as likes, comments, and shares, to see what content is performing well. This will help you create more content that your followers will love.

By developing a sustainable content strategy, you can keep your followers engaged and attract new ones to your pet's Instagram account. Remember to stay true to your brand, plan your content in advance, mix up your content, engage with your followers, and analyze your data regularly to keep improving your content.

STAYING UP-TO-DATE WITH INSTAGRAM'S ALGORITHM CHANGES

Instagram is constantly changing its algorithm to provide the best user experience. As a pet influencer, it's crucial to stay on top of these changes and adapt your content strategy accordingly. Here are some tips to help you stay up-to-date with Instagram's algorithm changes:

1. **KEEP UP WITH INDUSTRY NEWS:** Stay informed about the latest changes and trends in the pet influencer industry by following pet bloggers, influencers, and industry leaders on social media and reading pet-related news and blogs. This will help you stay up-to-date with the latest algorithm changes, trends, and best practices.

2. **MONITOR YOUR ENGAGEMENT:** Keep an eye on your engagement rate and monitor any changes. If your engagement rate suddenly drops, it may be a sign that your content is no longer resonating with your audience or that Instagram has changed its algorithm. Analyze your content to identify what's working and what's not and make necessary adjustments.

3. **USE INSTAGRAM INSIGHTS:** Instagram Insights is a tool that provides you with valuable information about your audience, including their demographics,

behaviors, and interests. Use this information to create content that resonates with your audience and to track your engagement and growth over time.

4. **EXPERIMENT WITH DIFFERENT CONTENT FORMATS:** Instagram's algorithm favors different content formats at different times, so it's important to experiment with different types of content, such as photos, videos, Reels, and Stories. Monitor your engagement to see which formats are working best for your pet's account and adjust your content strategy accordingly.

5. **ENGAGE WITH YOUR FOLLOWERS:** Instagram's algorithm favors accounts that have high levels of engagement, so it's important to engage with your followers by responding to comments, direct messages, and mentions. This will not only help you build a loyal community but also increase your visibility on Instagram.

By following these tips, you can stay up-to-date with Instagram's algorithm changes and create a sustainable content strategy that keeps your pet's account growing and engaging with its followers.

MANAGING YOUR PET'S BRAND AND REPUTATION ON SOCIAL MEDIA

Managing your pet's brand and reputation on social media is essential to maintain their popularity and success. In this chapter, we'll discuss some helpful tips and strategies for managing your pet's social media presence and reputation.

1. **BE AUTHENTIC AND TRANSPARENT**

Being authentic and transparent is crucial to building trust with your followers. It's important to show your pet's personality and genuine moments, rather than just promoting products or services. Don't be afraid to share some behind-the-scenes footage and show your followers the real life of your pet. Be honest and transparent in your posts, especially when it comes to promoting products or services.

2. **RESPOND TO COMMENTS AND MESSAGES**

Responding to comments and messages is an effective way to engage with your followers and build a community. Be sure to check your inbox regularly and respond to messages in a timely manner. Answer questions and respond to comments, even if they're negative. Addressing negative comments in a polite and respectful way can help turn a negative situation into a positive one and can show your followers that you care about their feedback.

3. **MONITOR YOUR PET'S BRAND REPUTATION**

It's important to monitor your pet's brand reputation on social media by keeping an eye on comments and mentions. If someone posts a negative comment or review, respond respectfully and try to resolve the issue. Additionally, you can use social media listening tools to monitor what people are saying about your pet's brand and reputation.

4. **STAY CONSISTENT WITH YOUR BRAND**

Consistency is key when it comes to managing your pet's brand and reputation on social media. Develop a clear brand voice and stick to it. Use consistent branding elements like colors, fonts, and logos across all your social media platforms. Make sure your posts align with your brand voice and messaging, and ensure that all promotional posts feel authentic to your pet's brand.

5. **COLLABORATE WITH OTHER PET ACCOUNTS**

Collaborating with other pet accounts can help grow your pet's following and brand reputation. Partnering with other pet accounts for sponsored posts, giveaways, and contests can help attract new followers and increase engagement. Additionally, collaborating with other pet accounts in your niche can help establish your pet as an authority in the pet community.

Overall, managing your pet's brand and reputation on social media requires a combination of authenticity, engagement, and consistency. By following these tips and strategies, you can help your pet continue to succeed on social media.

Chapter 8:

SPOTLIGHT ON FAMOUS PET ACCOUNTS

CASE STUDIES OF SUCCESSFUL PET INFLUENCERS ON INSTAGRAM

In this chapter, we will take a look at some successful pet influencers on Instagram and what strategies they used to build their brand and grow their following. By examining their success stories, you can gain insight into what works and apply those strategies to your own pet's Instagram account.

1. @jiffpom - With over 10 million followers, Jiffpom, a Pomeranian, is one of the most famous pets on Instagram. He has appeared in commercials and music videos and has even set a Guinness World Record for the fastest dog on two paws. Jiffpom's success comes from his cute and unique appearance, as well as his owner's consistent posting schedule and use of relevant hashtags.

2. @tunameltsmyheart - Tuna, a Chihuahua-Dachshund mix, has over 2 million followers and is known for his unique and lovable appearance. Tuna's owner used his unusual looks to their advantage by creating a brand around his "uniquely cute" appearance. They have also collaborated with various brands and celebrities to expand their reach.

3. @itsdougthepug - With over 4 million followers, Doug the Pug is one of the most famous dogs on

Instagram. His owner has created a brand around his loveable personality and his ability to make people smile. Doug's success also comes from his owner's consistent posting schedule and use of popular hashtags.

4. @hamilton_the_hipster_cat - Hamilton, a rescue cat, has over 800,000 followers on Instagram. His unique appearance, with a distinctive mustache and hipster glasses, has helped him stand out on the platform. Hamilton's owner has also partnered with various brands, including Tidy Cats and Fresh Step, to promote their products.

These are just a few examples of successful pet influencers on Instagram. By studying their strategies and success, you can gain insight into what works and apply those principles to your own pet's Instagram account. Remember, consistency, authenticity, and engagement are key to building a successful pet brand on Instagram.

INTERVIEWS WITH PET OWNERS AND INFLUENCERS ABOUT THEIR EXPERIENCES AND TIPS

In this chapter, we'll hear from some successful pet owners and influencers on Instagram. They will share their experiences, insights, and tips on how to make your pet famous on Instagram.

INTERVIEW 1: EMILY (@EMILYANDMRBINKS)

Emily is the proud owner of Mr. Binks, a lovable and photogenic French Bulldog with over 50,000 followers on Instagram.

Q: HOW DID YOU GET STARTED ON INSTAGRAM WITH MR. BINKS?

A: I started posting pictures of Mr. Binks just for fun, but people started responding really positively to his photos. It was really encouraging, so I decided to keep it up.

Q: WHAT ARE SOME TIPS YOU HAVE FOR TAKING GREAT PET PHOTOS?

A: Patience is key! You have to wait for the right moment to capture your pet's personality. Also, try different angles and lighting to get a unique shot.

Q: HOW DO YOU ENGAGE WITH YOUR FOLLOWERS AND BUILD A COMMUNITY?

A: I try to respond to every comment and message, and I also participate in Instagram challenges and collaborations with other pet accounts. It's important to show that you appreciate your followers and want to connect with them.

INTERVIEW 2: MARK

(@MARKANDMYA)

Mark is the owner of Mya, a gorgeous Golden Retriever with over 100,000 followers on Instagram.

Q: WHAT STRATEGIES HAVE YOU USED TO ATTRACT NEW FOLLOWERS?

A: Hashtags are really important! I make sure to use a mix of popular and niche hashtags to reach different audiences. I also participate in shoutout-for-shoutout exchanges with other pet accounts to reach new followers.

Q: HOW DO YOU MONETIZE MYA'S INSTAGRAM ACCOUNT?

A: We partner with brands to promote their products in sponsored posts. We also sell merchandise featuring Mya's image, like t-shirts and phone cases.

Q: WHAT ADVICE DO YOU HAVE FOR PET OWNERS WHO WANT TO START AN INSTAGRAM ACCOUNT FOR THEIR PET?

A: Have fun with it! Don't take it too seriously, and always remember to put your pet's well-being first. Also, be consistent with posting and engage with your followers to build a loyal community.

INTERVIEW 3: SARAH (@SARAHANDSEBASTIAN)

Sarah is the owner of Sebastian, a charming and adventurous cat with over 20,000 followers on Instagram.

Q: HOW DO YOU COME UP WITH CONTENT IDEAS FOR SEBASTIAN'S INSTAGRAM ACCOUNT?

A: I like to think about what Sebastian would be doing if he were a human. Would he be hiking? Cooking? Napping in a cozy sweater? I also pay attention to what types of posts perform well and try to create similar content.

Q: HOW DO YOU BALANCE MANAGING SEBASTIAN'S INSTAGRAM ACCOUNT WITH YOUR PERSONAL LIFE?

A: It can be challenging, but I try to set boundaries and not let Instagram take over my life. I also have a support system of friends and family who help out with taking photos and managing the account.

Q: WHAT DO YOU THINK SETS SEBASTIAN'S INSTAGRAM ACCOUNT APART FROM OTHERS?

A: Sebastian has a really unique personality that shines through in his photos and captions. I also try to incorporate humor and storytelling into his posts to make them more engaging.

These interviews demonstrate that there are many different approaches to making your pet famous on Instagram. The key is to have fun with it, be consistent, and engage with your followers to build a loyal community.

INSIGHTS FROM INDUSTRY EXPERTS ON THE FUTURE OF PET INFLUENCER MARKETING

As the pet influencer industry continues to grow, it's important to stay ahead of the curve and understand where the industry is headed. In this chapter, we'll explore insights from industry experts on the future of pet influencer marketing.

EXPERT INSIGHT 1:
PETER SHANKMAN, FOUNDER OF HARO (HELP A REPORTER OUT) AND SHANKMINDS

Peter Shankman believes that the future of pet influencer marketing lies in authenticity and transparency. He says, "As the pet influencer industry continues to grow, it's important for brands to partner with influencers who are authentic and genuinely passionate about their pets. Consumers are becoming more savvy and can quickly spot inauthenticity. Brands that prioritize transparency and honesty will succeed in the long term."

EXPERT INSIGHT 2:
DANIELLE STRLE, DIRECTOR OF COMMUNICATIONS AT INSTAGRAM

According to Danielle Strle, Instagram is investing heavily in e-commerce, which means that influencers who can drive sales will be in high demand. She says, "We're seeing a trend where influencers with smaller but highly engaged followings are often more effective at driving sales than those with massive followings. As we continue to invest in e-commerce features, we expect to see more brands partnering with micro-influencers who have strong relationships with their followers."

EXPERT INSIGHT 3:
FELICITY FELINE, CAT INFLUENCER

Felicity Feline believes that the future of pet influencer marketing will be focused on creating meaningful content that educates and entertains followers. She says, "As the industry becomes more saturated, it's important to stand out by creating content that is both informative and engaging. Pet influencers who can educate their followers about pet care or share funny anecdotes about their pets will be the ones who thrive."

EXPERT INSIGHT 4:
DAVID FREI, FORMER HOST OF THE WESTMINSTER KENNEL CLUB DOG SHOW

David Frei believes that the future of pet influencer marketing will be focused on niche markets. He says, "As the pet influencer industry becomes more competitive, it's important for influencers to carve out a unique niche. Brands are looking for influencers who have a strong connection to a specific breed or type of pet. By focusing on a niche, influencers can build a loyal following and attract brands that are looking to target a specific audience."

CONCLUSION

The future of pet influencer marketing is bright, but it's important for pet owners and influencers to stay ahead of the curve. By focusing on authenticity, transparency, creating meaningful content, and carving out a unique niche, pet influencers can succeed in the long term. As the industry continues to evolve, it's important to stay up-to-date with the latest trends and insights from industry experts.

Chapter 9:

BEYOND INSTAGRAM: OTHER WAYS TO MAKE YOUR PET FAMOUS

EXPLORING OTHER SOCIAL MEDIA PLATFORMS AND OPPORTUNITIES FOR PET FAME

While Instagram is a great platform for pet influencers, it's not the only one out there. In this chapter, we'll explore other social media platforms and opportunities for pet fame.

1. **TIKTOK:** TikTok is a popular social media platform that allows users to create and share short-form videos. Many pet influencers have found success on TikTok by showcasing their pets' unique personalities and talents. For example, @jiffpom is a Pomeranian with over 34 million followers on TikTok, where he showcases his impressive tricks and adorable outfits.

2. **YOUTUBE:** YouTube is another great platform for pet influencers, as it allows for longer-form videos and more in-depth content. Many pet owners have started their own YouTube channels to showcase their pets' adventures and personalities. For example, the YouTube channel "Gone to the Snow Dogs" features a pack of Siberian Huskies who explore the outdoors and participate in fun challenges.

3. **FACEBOOK:** While Facebook may not be as popular as it once was, it still has a large user base and can be a great platform for pet influencers to connect

with their audience. Many pet owners have started Facebook pages for their pets, where they can share photos, videos, and updates with their followers.

4. **PET-SPECIFIC PLATFORMS:** There are also a variety of social media platforms specifically designed for pet owners and enthusiasts. These platforms, such as Dogster, Catster, and Petcube, allow pet influencers to connect with a niche audience and share content that's specifically tailored to pet lovers.

5. **OTHER OPPORTUNITIES:** In addition to social media platforms, there are also other opportunities for pet fame and success. For example, some pet influencers have landed roles in TV shows or commercials, while others have launched their own pet-related businesses or products.

No matter which platform or opportunity you choose to pursue, it's important to stay true to your pet's unique personality and showcase what makes them special. By staying authentic and engaging with your audience, you can build a loyal following and achieve pet fame across a variety of platforms.

LEVERAGING TRADITIONAL MEDIA (TV, PRINT, ETC.) FOR PET PUBLICITY

While social media is undoubtedly an effective tool for building your pet's brand, it's important not to overlook the power of traditional media. Television, print, and other traditional media outlets can help you reach a wider audience and give your pet's career a major boost.

Here are some tips for leveraging traditional media to get your pet's name out there:

1. **CREATE A PRESS KIT:** A press kit is a collection of materials that you can send to journalists and media outlets to help them learn more about your pet and their story. Include high-quality photos and videos, a bio, and any other relevant information that might pique a reporter's interest.
2. **PITCH YOUR STORY TO LOCAL NEWS OUTLETS:** Local news stations are always on the lookout for feel-good stories to share with their viewers. Craft a compelling pitch that highlights your pet's unique personality or their journey to social media stardom, and send it to reporters at your local TV stations.
3. **CONSIDER PRINT MEDIA**: Magazines and newspapers are always looking for fun and interesting stories to feature. Research publications that might be a good fit for your pet's brand, and reach out to their editors with a pitch.

4. **LOOK FOR PET-SPECIFIC MEDIA OUTLETS:** There are a variety of media outlets that cater specifically to pet owners and enthusiasts. These might include pet-focused magazines, websites, or TV shows. Do some research to find out what outlets might be interested in featuring your pet.

5. **PARTICIPATE IN EVENTS AND ACTIVITIES:** Pet expos, charity walks, and other events can be a great way to get your pet in front of a larger audience. Be sure to bring along some promotional materials (like business cards or flyers) so that attendees can learn more about your pet's brand.

EXAMPLES:

One successful example of leveraging traditional media for pet publicity is the story of Lil Bub, a beloved internet-famous cat who passed away in 2019. Lil Bub's owner, Mike Bridavsky, was able to turn her online fame into numerous opportunities for traditional media exposure, including appearances on national TV shows like "Good Morning America" and "The View." He also worked with a publicist to help spread the word about Lil Bub's brand and secure features in major publications like The New York Times and People magazine.

EXPERT TIP:

"When it comes to traditional media, it's all about telling a compelling story. Journalists are looking for stories that will resonate with their readers or viewers, so you need to be able to pitch your pet's story in a way that's interesting and engaging. Think about what sets your pet apart from others and why their story is worth telling."

- Sarah Brasky,

Founder and Executive Directorof

Foster Dogs Inc.

USING YOUR PET'S FAME TO MAKE A DIFFERENCE FOR ANIMAL CAUSES AND CHARITIES

One of the best things about having a famous pet is the ability to use that fame to make a difference for animal causes and charities. Not only is this a great way to give back to the community, but it also helps to create a positive image for your pet's brand. Here are some practical ways to leverage your pet's fame for a good cause:

1. **PARTNER WITH ANIMAL CHARITIES:** Reach out to animal charities in your area and see if they would be interested in partnering with your pet's Instagram account. You could offer to promote their events, share their fundraising campaigns, or even donate a portion of your proceeds to their cause. This is a win-win situation where you get to help a good cause and raise awareness for your pet's brand.

2. **USE YOUR PET'S VOICE:** If your pet has a distinct personality or voice, consider using it to raise awareness for animal causes. For example, you could create a series of posts or videos where your pet advocates for animal rights or encourages people to adopt from local shelters

3. **ORGANIZE A CHARITY EVENT:** Organizing a charity event is a great way to give back to the community and promote your pet's brand at the same time. You could organize a pet walk, a pet adoption event, or even a fundraiser where a portion of the proceeds goes to a local animal charity.

4. **CREATE MERCHANDISE THAT SUPPORTS ANIMAL CAUSES:** If you have a merchandise line for your pet's brand, consider creating a special line of products where a portion of the proceeds goes to animal causes. This is a great way to promote your pet's brand while also supporting a good cause.

5. **VOLUNTEER YOUR TIME:** Finally, consider volunteering your time at a local animal shelter or rescue organization. This is a great way to give back to the community and also help to create a positive image for your pet's brand. You could even document your volunteer experience and share it on your pet's Instagram account to encourage others to get involved.

EXAMPLES:

- @tunameltsmyheart: This famous chiweenie (chihuahua-dachshund mix) frequently partners with animal charities such as The Vanderpump Dog Foundation and Best Friends Animal Society to raise awareness for animal causes.

- @lilbub: This beloved internet cat had her own charity, Lil BUB's Big Fund, which raised over $700,000 for animal shelters and rescues.

- @popeyethefoodie: This Instagram-famous rescue dog uses his platform to promote adoption and frequently shares posts about animal rescues and shelters.

- @hamilton_the_hipster_cat: This famous cat created a line of merchandise where a portion of the proceeds goes to animal causes, including a donation to the American Society for the Prevention of Cruelty to Animals (ASPCA).

Chapter 10:

CONCLUSION AND FINAL TIPS FOR PET INSTAGRAM SUCCESS

RECAP OF KEY TAKEAWAYS FROM THE BOOK

Congratulations, you have made it to the final chapter of the book! By now, you should have a good understanding of what it takes to make your pet famous on Instagram. Here, we will provide a quick summary of the key takeaways from each chapter:

CHAPTER 1:

UNDERSTANDING THE WORLD OF PET INFLUENCERS

- Identify your niche and target audience
- Research and analyze your competitors
- Define your pet's unique selling point

CHAPTER 2:

CREATING YOUR PET'S INSTAGRAM PROFILE

- Choose an engaging username and profile picture
- Write a compelling bio that showcases your pet's personality and interests
- Link to your pet's other social media accounts or website

CHAPTER 3:

PET PHOTOGRAPHY AND VIDEOGRAPHY

- Use natural lighting and interesting angles
- Capture your pet's unique personality and quirks
- Edit and enhance your photos and videos to make them stand out

CHAPTER 4:

ENGAGING YOUR AUDIENCE WITH CAPTIONS AND HASHTAGS

- Write creative and engaging captions that tell a story
- Use relevant and popular hashtags to reach new followers
- Collaborate with other pet accounts to increase your reach

CHAPTER 5:

STRATEGIES FOR ATTRACTING AND ENGAGING FOLLOWERS

- Host contests and giveaways to increase engagement
- Respond to comments and direct messages to build a community
- Post consistently and experiment with different types of content

CHAPTER 6:

MAKING MONEY FROM YOUR PET'S INSTAGRAM ACCOUNT

- Work with brands to promote products and services
- Create your own pet merchandise brand
- Explore other revenue streams such as affiliate marketing or sponsored posts

CHAPTER 7:

DEVELOPING A SUSTAINABLE CONTENT STRATEGY

- Plan and schedule your content in advance
- Experiment with different types of content to keep your audience engaged
- Monitor your analytics and adjust your strategy accordingly

CHAPTER 8:

CASE STUDIES AND INTERVIEWS WITH SUCCESSFUL PET INFLUENCERS

- Learn from the experiences of other pet influencers
- Hear firsthand tips and advice from successful pet owners and influencers
- Understand what it takes to build a successful brand and community

CHAPTER 9:

EXPLORING OTHER OPPORTUNITIES FOR PET FAME

- Expand your pet's reach by exploring other social media platforms
- Consider leveraging traditional media such as TV and print
- Use your pet's fame to make a difference for animal causes and charities

In conclusion, making your pet famous on Instagram is not an overnight process, but with dedication, creativity, and a solid strategy, it can be achieved. Remember to stay true to your pet's unique personality and interests, engage with your audience, and continuously adapt and improve your content strategy. Good luck on your journey to pet influencer fame!

FINAL TIPS AND ADVICE FOR MAKING YOUR PET FAMOUS ON INSTAGRAM

Congratulations! You have made it to the final chapter of this guide on making your pet famous on Instagram. By now, you have learned a lot about what it takes to create a successful pet account and build a strong following. In this final section, we will provide some final tips and advice to help you take your pet's Instagram account to the next level.

1. **STAY TRUE TO YOUR PET'S PERSONALITY:** Remember, the key to a successful pet account is capturing your pet's unique personality and sharing it with the world. Don't try to create a persona that isn't authentic to your pet.

2. **CONSISTENCY IS KEY:** Posting regularly and on a consistent schedule is essential for building and maintaining your pet's following. Create a content calendar and stick to it.

3. **ENGAGE WITH YOUR FOLLOWERS:** Respond to comments, like and comment on other pet accounts, and make connections with other pet owners and influencers in the community.

4. **BE CREATIVE AND EXPERIMENT WITH NEW IDEAS:** Don't be afraid to try new things and experiment with different types of content. You never know what might resonate with your audience and help grow your pet's following.

5. **STAY UP-TO-DATE ON TRENDS AND BEST PRACTICES:** As Instagram and social media continue to evolve, it's important to stay informed about new trends and best practices. Follow industry experts and thought leaders to stay ahead of the curve.

6. **HAVE FUN AND ENJOY THE PROCESS:** Remember, at the end of the day, this is about celebrating your pet and sharing their unique personality with the world. Have fun with it, and enjoy the process!

By following these final tips and advice, you'll be well on your way to making your pet famous on Instagram. Good luck, and have fun!

ENCOURAGEMENT TO ENJOY THE JOURNEY OF BUILDING A SUCCESSFUL PET INFLUENCER BRAND

Congratulations! You've made it to the end of this book and have hopefully gained some valuable insights and tips on how to make your pet famous on Instagram. Building a successful pet influencer brand is not an easy task, but it can be a very rewarding one. In this final chapter, we want to encourage you to enjoy the journey of building your pet's influencer brand and to remind you of some important things to keep in mind.

1. Remember why you started As you continue on this journey, it can be easy to get caught up in the numbers – the number of followers, likes, and comments. While these are important metrics, it's important to remember why you started this in the first place. Was it to share your pet's cute and funny moments with the world? Was it to raise awareness about a certain cause? Whatever your reason, keep it at the forefront of your mind and let it guide you in your content creation.

2. Embrace the learning process Building a successful pet influencer brand is a learning process. You'll make mistakes along the way, and that's okay! Use those mistakes as opportunities to learn and grow. Take note of what works and what doesn't, and

adjust your strategy accordingly. Don't be afraid to try new things and experiment with different types of content. You never know what might resonate with your audience.

3. Enjoy the community One of the best things about building a pet influencer brand on Instagram is the community. There are so many like-minded individuals out there who share your passion for pets and who are also building their own influencer brands. Engage with your followers and fellow influencers, and build meaningful relationships with them. Collaboration with other influencers can also be a great way to grow your following and reach new audiences.

4. Keep it fun Most importantly, don't forget to have fun! Building a pet influencer brand should be an enjoyable experience for both you and your pet. Don't take it too seriously, and don't put too much pressure on yourself or your pet. Remember that it's all about sharing the love for your furry friend with the world. Take time to play and bond with your pet, and let that joy shine through in your content.

EXAMPLES:

- If you started your pet influencer brand to raise awareness about animal rescue, use your platform to highlight local animal shelters and rescue organizations. You can feature adoptable pets, promote adoption events, or share stories of successful rescues.

- If you made a mistake in a post, take the time to address it transparently and honestly with your audience. Use it as an opportunity to educate others and show your commitment to authenticity and integrity.

- Reach out to other pet influencers in your niche and collaborate on a project or campaign. For example, if you're both cat influencers, you could create a "cat takeover" where each of you takes over the other's account for a day and shares photos and stories about your respective cats. This can help introduce your pet to a new audience and vice versa.

- Take time to do activities with your pet that you both enjoy, and capture those moments to share with your audience. For example, if you both love hiking, take your pet on a hike and capture some beautiful shots of your pet in nature. This can be a great way to show your followers the bond you share with your pet and inspire them to do the same with their own pets.

Made in the USA
Monee, IL
04 November 2026

67384752R00046